ENRIQUE IGLESIAS

A Real-Life Reader Biography

Christine Granados

Mitchell Lane Publishers, Inc.
P.O. Box 619
Bear, Delaware 19701

First Printing

Real-Life Reader Biographies

Selena	Robert Rodriguez	Mariah Carey	Rafael Palmeiro
Tommy Nuñez	Trent Dimas	Cristina Saralegui	Andres Galarraga
Oscar De La Hoya	Gloria Estefan	Jimmy Smits	Mary Joe Fernandez
Cesar Chavez	Chuck Norris	Sinbad	Paula Abdul
Vanessa Williams	Celine Dion	Mia Hamm	Sammy Sosa
Brandy	Michelle Kwan	Rosie O'Donnell	Shania Twain
Garth Brooks	Jeff Gordon	Mark McGwire	Salma Hayek
Sheila E.	Hollywood Hogan	Ricky Martin	Britney Spears
Arnold Schwarzenegger	Jennifer Lopez	Kobe Bryant	Derek Jeter
Steve Jobs	Sandra Bullock	Julia Roberts	Robin Williams
Jennifer Love Hewitt	Keri Russell	Sarah Michelle Gellar	Liv Tyler
Melissa Joan Hart	Drew Barrymore	Alicia Silverstone	Katie Holmes
Winona Ryder	Alyssa Milano	Freddie Prinze, Jr.	**Enrique Iglesias**
Christina Aguilera			

Library of Congress Cataloging-in-Publication Data
Granados, Christine, 1969-
    Enrique Iglesias/Christine Granados.
      p. cm. — (A real-life reader biography)
    ISBN 1-58415-045-9
    1. Iglesias, Enrique, vocalist—Juvenile literature. 2. Singers—Biography—Juvenile literature. [1. Iglesias, Enrique, vocalist. 2. Singers. 3. Hispanic Americans—Biography.] I. Title. II. Series.
ML3930.I39 G73 2000
782.42164'092—dc21
[B]
                                                        00-057711

ABOUT THE AUTHOR: Christine Granados has been a writer and editor for many years. She was recently the editor of *Moderna* magazine and has been a newspaper reporter for *The El Paso Times, Austin American-Statesman,* and *Long Beach Press-Telegram.* She is a contributing author to the Contemporary American Success Stories series (Mitchell Lane), authored *Rosie O'Donnell* (Mitchell Lane) and *Sheila E.* (Mitchell Lane) and has published numerous magazine feature stories.
PHOTO CREDITS: Cover: Reuters/Jill Connelly/Archive Photos; p. 4 Scott Harrison/Archive Photos; p. 7 AP Photo/Asamu Honda; p. 20 AP Photo/John Riley; p. 23 Reuters/Claudio Papi/Archive Photos; p. 26 Reuters/Mike Segar/Archive Photos; p. 27 Tim Mosenfelder/Corbis; p. 29 Fitzroy Barrett/Globe Photos
ACKNOWLEDGMENTS: The following story has been thoroughly researched, and to the best of our knowledge, represents a true story. While every possible effort has been made to ensure accuracy, the publisher will not assume liability for damages caused by inaccuracies in the data, and makes no warranty on the accuracy of the information contained herein. This story has not been authorized by Enrique Iglesias or any of his representatives.

Table of Contents

Chapter 1
The Hard Way

Enrique Iglesias, a world famous pop singer, is not the kind of person who takes the easy road, although he has had many opportunities to do so. After all, he is the son Julio Iglesias, an internationally known singer and millionaire. Enrique could have used his father's fame and money to advance his own career as a singer/songwriter, but instead he chose to work hard for his success.

When Enrique went shopping for a record label to record his music he did not want to use his father's name to

> Enrique Iglesias is not the kind of person who takes the easy road.

open doors. He wanted to succeed using his own talents. His father's former manager Fernan Martinez, who became Enrique's manager, told him not to make life so hard for himself. "I said, 'Why do you want to take the hard way?' We have the easiest way," Martinez told Richard Harrington of *The Washington Post*. Still, Enrique insisted that they not use his father's name at all when looking for a record deal. So Enrique Iglesias of Spain became Enrique Martinez from Columbia who wanted to sing. "He didn't want to be played on the radio because he was Julio Iglesias's son," said Fernan Martinez in a *Teen People* interview. "When he was little, if a friend introduced him as Julio Iglesias's son, he would walk away. He would rather not get into a disco than say he was Julio Iglesias's son. He never used that, either in school, or with girls or in a restaurant."

Enrique also kept his ambitions private. When he was fifteen years old

Enrique's father, Julio, is a famous, international singer.

When
Enrique
was a
sophomore
in college,
he decided
music was
going to be
his future.

he would spend hours each day after high school in a friend's basement singing and writing songs. "The songs were real cheesy," Enrique said in *The Washington Post*. "I used to cry about how bad they sounded. That was the hardest part, getting used to my voice, getting used to feeling good about what I was singing and writing. It took a long time."

He continued writing and singing in secret until 1994 when he knew he was ready to go for his goal. He called Martinez. At the time, he was a sophomore in college at the University of Miami majoring in business. He decided music was going to be his future. Although he didn't want to use his father's name for access, he didn't want to tell his father or mother that he was going to drop out of college to pursue his dream, either.

"It hurt me to keep a secret from my parents," Enrique told Peter Castro, in a *People* magazine interview. "But if I hadn't, I wouldn't be where I am now."

All the major U.S. record labels passed on Enrique Martinez. "Actually, with some companies I used my real name," Enrique told Jancee Dunn in a *Rolling Stone* interview. "I got rejected with both. But I didn't get discouraged, because I didn't know what it felt like to be successful. Everyone gets rejected— record companies, a lot of times, are so blind." It wasn't until one year later that a small record label called Fonovisa that specializes in Mexican music signed Enrique. By then he was using his real last name; but, he was also being recognized for his own talent.

When his father found out about his son's plans he was not happy. Enrique recalled in *People* magazine, "My father and I spoke when he found out, and he was shocked. I told him I was sorry. I said, 'Look, this is exactly what I've always wanted to do. Just let me do it my way, please.'"

A small record label called Fonovisa that specializes in Mexican music signed Enrique.

Chapter 2
Family Life

Although he was born in Spain, Enrique considers himself mainly American.

Enrique Iglesias Preysler was born May 8, 1975, to Julio Iglesias and Isabel Preysler in Madrid, Spain. He is the youngest son of Julio and Isabel. Enrique has an older sister, Chabeli, 28, a TV news reporter and an older brother, Julio Jose, 27, a model-turned actor. Julio Iglesias is an internationally known singer born and raised in Spain. Isabel is a journalist who was born into a wealthy family in the Philippines. People consider Enrique Latino, because he was born in Spain and speaks fluent Spanish. He is also half Asian, because his mother is from the Philippines. But, Enrique considers himself mainly American. He has lived in Miami, Florida, since he was seven years old. "It's funny because I'm completely mixed, but in a way I feel like I'm Latino, because I grew up in Miami with Latino friends," Enrique said in a *Rolling Stone* interview. "And at the same time I feel Asian, and at the same time I feel like I understand American culture because I grew up in the U.S. I think I have the best of the three worlds."

When Enrique was small, he lived in a mansion in Spain under the constant glare of television crews and photographers, who wanted to get photographs of the superstar Spanish singer Julio Iglesias's family. Although his father's success as a Latin music singer afforded the Iglesias family a large mansion with nannies and servants, the music kept Dad away from home. Enrique's parents divorced when he was just three years old; and, in 1979, his

When Enrique was small, he lived in a mansion in Spain under the constant glare of television crews and photographers.

father moved from Madrid to Miami, Florida.

In 1982, Julio Iglesias' fame became dangerous when Enrique's grandfather was kidnapped and held for ransom in Spain. Fearing for their lives, Isabel sent her two sons to live with their father in Miami. "My family was afraid that someone would kidnap my brother or me," Enrique told Betty Cortina of *People en Español*, the Spanish language edition of *People* magazine. (Their grandfather was eventually saved by a rescue operation.) Enrique remembers the move as an adventure.   He said in a *Rolling Stone* interview: "It was sad when my grandfather was kidnapped, but then he was rescued, and once he was rescued it became like a movie. I remember coming to the U.S. in a huge plane, and when it landed in Miami, there were FBI agents everywhere, and we were getting picked up by helicopters, and I was like 'Whoa, cool.' Once I got here, I missed all my friends from Spain, and my mother, and it was pretty

In 1982, Enrique's grand-father was kidnapped and held for ransom in Spain.

hard. I used to cry every single day." Enrique's mother, Isabel said in *People* magazine, "It broke my heart to send them away but we had to for security reasons. If I had known [at the time] that their father wasn't around [much], it might have been different."

Isabel meant that Julio's work schedule had often kept him away from the Miami mansion. Enrique put his father's fame in perspective in a *People en Español* interview, "Sure, I knew I was the son of Julio. But it really wasn't important to me. It wasn't like he was a rock star that all my friends knew." Rather, Julio Iglesias was a singer of romantic, slow songs that he sang in Spanish.

With his mother in another country and his father rarely home, Enrique got lonely, but he made the best of the situation. "I did miss them, but you get used to seeing your Dad maybe once a month," Enrique said in a *People* interview. "There was a lot of communication between us, which helped a lot."

With his mother in another country and his father rarely home, Enrique got lonely, but he made the best of the situation.

He credits the woman who raised him for keeping his feet on the ground. Elvira Olivares, more like a second mother than a nanny, raised Enrique and Julio Jose. "I had to be home by eleven at night and I had an allowance. I wasn't a spoiled kid," Enrique said in *People en Español*. In fact, Elvira still lives with Enrique in the home he was raised in. "I hate saying the word 'nanny.' She took care of us when were little. [Now] she is my friend," he said.

Chapter 3
Laying the Groundwork

The move from Spain to the United States was hard on Enrique, and he tended to act up in elementary school. He was suspended from school in third grade for putting a lizard on his teacher's back. However, by junior high school his conduct was under control. As a freshman in high school he was the shortest guy in school and very shy. At the time, he was five-foot, four-inches tall, but eventually he grew to be six-foot, two-inches tall. "I was so ugly that no one would date me," he said in a *People en Español* interview. In the same interview, he said he was devastated

Enrique was suspended from school for putting a lizard on his teacher's back.

when a girl he asked to the prom cancelled on him. "I cried for a week," he said. "In high school I probably got rejected seventy percent of the time," he told Dunn of *Rolling Stone*. "I was too skinny and small. I ended up going to the prom by myself." His good friend, Andrés Restrepo, was nicer when he described Enrique as a kid. "He wasn't part of the popular group [in high school]," Andres told *People en Español*.

It was in high school at Gulliver Preparatory School in Miami that Enrique started to think about a career in music. Every day after school when he was fifteen years old he would spend hours holed up in Roberto Morales' basement studio working on songs. Roberto was an older musician who performed in Miami restaurants. "I was a very independent kid," Enrique told Charles Gibson, the host of ABC's *Good Morning America*. "To me, music was like therapy. I was a very shy kid too, so I used to hide in my bedroom and just write all day and all night. And I didn't want to tell anyone. It was like my little secret. It was like a diary. . . . I didn't want that secret exposed."

He didn't want to tell anyone because by then, he was already in his second year of college at the University of Miami. If his secret was exposed, his parents would have tried to stop him from leaving college. Finally, he had to tell someone, and that someone was Fernan Martinez, his father's former manager. He proved to be the right person. When Enrique invited Martinez to the basement to hear his songs, Martinez was blown away. "It was beautiful, the expression, the eyes, the hands, the body," Martinez said in *The Washington Post*. "You could see how much he believed in what he was singing." That day Martinez heard five songs—three in English and two in Spanish. He told Enrique he should follow in his father's footsteps and sing songs only in Spanish. But Enrique made it clear he wanted no connection with his father in getting into the music

When Enrique invited Martinez to the basement to hear his songs, Martinez was blown away.

business. Although he did not use his father's name to get started, he did take Martinez's advice and sang only Spanish songs. It was Elvira who loaned him the $5,000 to record his first demo (audition tape) when he 17 years old.

Chapter 4
Fame on His Own Terms

After one year of countless rejections by record labels, Enrique was picked up by a small record label out of California called Fonovisa that specialized in Mexican music. He recorded his first album titled *Enrique Iglesias* in 1995 when he was just twenty years old.

When Enrique's father found out about the recording contract he was not happy about it. But Julio Iglesias soon warmed to the idea and is now a proud Dad. "I told him to do as he wishes, but do it well because this is something very serious," Julio Iglesias said in an interview. "I'm trying to work with him...

Enrique recorded his first album in 1995 when he was just twenty years old.

At first, Enrique did not want anyone to know about his talent.

advise him on things such as accepting offers too quickly. But he's listening with a deaf ear." Enrique said he respects his father and although he did not want any help from him, he learned a lot just by growing up with him. "I feel like I'm a step ahead, from growing up with my father, in the sense of learning to surround myself with good people," Enrique said in a *Rolling Stone* interview. "As a little kid, I could tell the people who really loved my father and who didn't. As a kid, you can actually distinguish really well."

Enrique's first record was an instant success. It sold over 5.8 million copies and won him the Grammy for Best Latin Pop Performer in 1996. Because Enrique is forever grateful to the woman who raised him as her own, he dedicated his debut album to Elvira. "She gave part of her life to us. She filled that gap," he said in *People*. Elvira, proud of Enrique, said in the same *People* interview, "I have never had chil-

Enrique's first record sold over 5.8 million copies and won him the Grammy for Best Latin Pop Performer in 1996.

Eight of Enrique's songs on his first two albums have been number one on the *Billboard* Magazine list in the United States and in eighteen other countries.

dren, but the love I have given these children has been a mother's."

Enrique's second album, *Vivir*, proved to be just as successful. *Vivir*, which means, "Live" in English, sold over five million copies throughout the world. He earned two platinum records for both albums. Eight of his songs on his first two albums have been number one on the *Billboard* Magazine list in the United States and in eighteen other countries. He recorded his third album, *Cosas del Amor* (Love Things) in 1998. The same year Enrique was named *People en Espanol's* Sexiest Man in the World. He recorded all three albums in Spanish but also cut tracks in Italian and Portuguese. In all, he sold thirteen million copies of his first three albums. "His first prize was a Grammy," said Martinez in a *Teen People* interview. "His first live [TV] show was on David Letterman. He starts where most people want to arrive! He's so effective; like the batters who always hit a home run."

Although it was not what his parents wanted for him, Enrique pursued a career as a singer.

The next step for Enrique was to record songs in English.

The next step for Enrique was to record songs in English. "After all," he explained to a reporter from *The Miami Herald*, "I've grown up in the U.S. I used to write in English. My first demo was in English. The first time my manager ever heard me was in English." He told a reporter with *The Washington Post* that he never listened to his father's music when he was growing up. "I used to listen to a lot of Anglo acts—Fleetwood Mac, Dire Straits, Billy Joel, Journey, John Mellencamp." So it was only natural that he model his music after the songs he grew up listening to.

Chapter 5
A New Path

His first English-language single *Bailamos* (We Dance) was destined to become a hit. Enrique recorded the song after someone from Universal Records played it for him over the telephone. "I don't usually hear other people's songs, but as soon I heard it, I said, 'Oh my God, I love it,'" Enrique said in *Billboard* Magazine. "It was sent over to my house, and in a minute I said, 'Let's go into the studio and do it.' I didn't even have an English label, but I had to record it."

A few months later, the actor Will Smith called Enrique. Smith was a fan

"I don't usually hear other people's songs, but as soon as I heard it, I said, 'Oh my God, I love it.'"

Enrique performs at the VH1 "Men Strike Back" concert.

of Enrique and he asked him if he would like to contribute a song for the soundtrack of his new movie *Wild Wild West*.

"I sent over the song [*Bailamos*], and Interscope picked it up," Enrique said in *Billboard*. "I never even thought it would be released in the U.S., and I certainly didn't think it would become a single. When stuff happens like that, it's definitely for a reason."

The song became a number one hit single in English, and the Universal/Interscope record label picked him up when his contract with Fonovisa ex-

Enrique never thought that Bailamos *would be released in the U.S.*

pired. He signed a $44 million, six-album record deal. Three albums were to be recorded in Spanish and three in English.

"Enrique has the power and charisma to move people," Jimmy Iovine, co-owner of Interscope told *Billboard* Magazine. "Every now and then, you find someone who is just very natural, who comes off like he owns it. It has nothing to do with the fact that he's a Latin artist. He's just a great artist."

His first English language album for Universal/Interscope came on the heels of the single *Bailamos'* success. His album titled *Enrique* sold five millions copies worldwide. On the album he recorded a duet, *Could I Have This Kiss Forever?* with Whitney Houston. When Enrique first heard the song he asked Arista Record founder Clive Davis if he could have the song for his album. "Clive said, 'Well, Whitney Houston likes it, too. Why don't you guys do it together?'" Enrique also included Bruce Springsteen's song *Sad Eyes* on the al-

Enrique's album *Enrique* included a duet with Whitney Houston.

bum. "I love Bruce Springsteen," Enrique said in *The Orange County Register* interview. "I think it is a great song for people to get to know. But what are the critics going to say? 'He goes and crosses over and now he's going to record a Bruce Springsteen song.' But the truth is that I went in the studio, tried it and thought, 'If I like it, it'll work. If not, then we don't include it on the album.'"

There seems to be no end to

Enrique won an American Music Award in 1999.

There seems to be no end to Enrique's success, and he loves it.

Enrique's success, and he loves it. "I'm in a privileged position right now, and just being able to do what I love is amazing," he told MTV's Carson Daly in a *YM Magazine* interview. "But if I'm married in ten years, I might just stay in the studio producing for other people. I'd like to do that at some point. But right now I want to go as far as I can as a performer." For a talented, hard worker like Enrique Iglesias, the sky is the limit.

Discography

2000	*The Best Hits*	Fonovisa
1999	*Enrique*	Interscope Records
1998	*Cosas Del Amor*	Fonovisa
1997	*Vivir*	Fonovisa
1995	*Enrique Iglesias*	Fonovisa

Chronology

Index